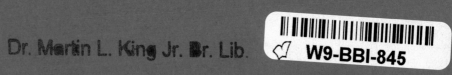

Alphabet Books

African Animals ABC

An Alphabet Safari

by Sarah L. Schuette

Consultant:
Brandie Smith
Assistant Director, Conservation and Science
American Zoo and Aquarium Association

Capstone *press*

Mankato, Minnesota

A is for aardvark.

Aardvarks live in burrows that they dig with their claws. Using their long, sticky tongues, aardvarks catch termites and ants.

Aa Bb Cc Dd Ee Ff Gg Hh Ii Jj Kk Ll Mm
Nn Oo Pp Qq Rr Ss Tt Uu Vv Ww Xx Yy Zz

B is for bushbaby.

Bushbabies sleep in trees
during the day. At night, they
jump from branch to branch.

C is for cheetah.

Cheetahs are fast. It takes a
cheetah about six seconds to run
the length of two football fields.

Aa Bb Cc Dd Ee Ff Gg Hh Ii Jj Kk Ll Mm Nn Oo Pp Qq Rr Ss Tt Uu Vv Ww Xx Yy Zz

D is for **d**warf mongoose.

A dwarf mongoose looks like a squirrel. It hunts for crickets, termites, and grasshoppers.

E is for elephant.

African elephants are the biggest land animals on Earth. Elephants flap their ears to cool off.

F is for fish eagle.

Fish eagles live near water. They catch fish with their strong claws.

Aa Bb Cc Dd Ee Ff Gg Hh Ii Jj Kk Ll Mm Nn Oo Pp Qq Rr Ss Tt Uu Vv Ww Xx Yy Zz

G is for giraffe.

Giraffes use their long necks
to reach leaves on tall trees.
They even sleep standing up.

H is for hippopotamus.

Hippos spend most of their time in water. They can stay underwater for about six minutes.

Aa Bb Cc Dd Ee Ff Gg **Hh** Ii Jj Kk Ll Mm Nn Oo Pp Qq Rr Ss Tt Uu Vv Ww Xx Yy Zz

I is for impala.

Male impalas show off by locking horns with other males. Female impalas do not have horns.

Aa Bb Cc Dd Ee Ff Gg Hh Ii Jj Kk Ll Mm Nn Oo Pp Qq Rr Ss Tt Uu Vv Ww Xx Yy Zz

J is for jackal.

Jackals live together in pairs. They look like small dogs and are very noisy.

K is for kudu.

Kudus have large, twisting horns. While running, kudus tip their heads back so their horns do not get stuck in trees.

L is for lion.

Lions rest most of the day. They
live in groups called prides.

M is for mountain gorilla.

Mountain gorillas love to eat. They sometimes spend three hours eating a breakfast of berries, bamboo, and leaves.

N is for Nile monitor.

Nile monitors are one of the biggest lizards in the world. They often live near water and eat crocodile eggs.

Aa Bb Cc Dd Ee Ff Gg Hh Ii Jj Kk Ll Mm **Nn** Oo Pp Qq Rr Ss Tt Uu Vv Ww Xx Yy Zz

O is for ostrich.

Ostriches are birds, but they cannot
fly. Instead, ostriches run very quickly
to get where they want to go.

Aa Bb Cc Dd Ee Ff Gg Hh Ii Jj Kk Ll Mm Nn Oo Pp Qq Rr Ss Tt Uu Vv Ww Xx Yy Zz

P is for **p**angolin.

Pangolins are covered with hard scales. They stay safe by rolling themselves into balls.

Q is for squacco heron.

Squacco herons build nests out of sticks. They lay green eggs.

R is for rhinoceros.

African rhinos have
horns made out of hair.
Each rhino has two
horns on its snout.

S is for spotted hyena.

Spotted hyenas live in groups called clans.

They are good hunters and scavengers.

Aa Bb Cc Dd Ee Ff Gg Hh Ii Jj Kk Ll Mm Nn Oo Pp Qq Rr **Ss** Tt Uu Vv Ww Xx Yy Zz

T is for tortoise.

Tortoises are large turtles that live on land. Some tortoises can live to be more than 100 years old.

U is for usambara tarantula.

Usambara tarantulas catch and eat insects.
When scared, they lift their front legs and
show their fangs.

Aa Bb Cc Dd Ee Ff Gg Hh Ii Jj Kk Ll Mm Nn Oo Pp Qq Rr Ss Tt **Uu** Vv Ww Xx Yy Zz

V is for vervet monkey.

Vervet monkeys have very sharp teeth for eating plants and insects. They jump around and make loud noises when they see danger.

W is for warthog.

Warthogs are large pigs with warts and tusks. Warthogs use their strong snouts to dig for food.

X is for oxpecker.

Oxpeckers have strong red or yellow beaks.
They eat ticks and fleas off the bodies of
water buffalo, elephants, giraffes, and
other animals.

Aa Bb Cc Dd Ee Ff Gg Hh Ii Jj Kk Ll Mm
Nn Oo Pp Qq Rr Ss Tt Uu Vv Ww Xx Yy Zz

Y is for yellow baboon.

Yellow baboons do not always get along with each other. Male baboons will fight another baboon about once a month.

Z is for Zebra.

Zebras look like horses with stripes. Each zebra
has its own pattern of stripes.

Aa Bb Cc Dd Ee Ff Gg Hh Ii Jj Kk Ll Mm Nn Oo Pp Qq Rr Ss Tt Uu Vv Ww Xx Yy Zz

African Animal Facts

Aardvark
- has a long, sticky tongue
- catches insects at night

Bushbaby
- hops like a kangaroo
- moves around at night

Cheetah
- hunts during the day
- known as the fastest land animal

Dwarf mongoose
- lives in groups of 10 to 40 members
- sleeps in a den

Elephant
- lives in Africa and Asia
- eats up to 18 hours a day

Fish eagle
- makes a nest out of large sticks
- uses the same nest every year

Giraffe
- gallops quickly
- is the tallest animal living on land

Hippopotamus
- does not sweat
- uses mud to keep cool

Impala
- grazes on grass
- eats leaves off of trees

Jackal
- eats insects, reptiles, mammals, and plants
- has three species in Africa

Kudu
- leaps very high when scared
- females are smaller than males

Lion
- is the second largest cat (tiger is the largest)
- has a mane (male only)

Mountain gorilla
- sleeps in nests of grass
- members of the ape family

Nile monitor
- has a forked tongue
- uses its tail as a weapon

Ostrich

- lays very large eggs
- takes turns sitting on eggs

Pangolin

- has no teeth
- eats at night

Squacco heron

- eats fish, frogs, and insects
- feeding of chicks done by both adults

Rhinoceros

- rolls in mud and dust to protect skin
- does not sweat

Spotted hyena

- lives in a group called a clan
- makes a spooky, laughing call

Tortoise

- lays eggs
- has many types living in Africa

Usambara tarantula

- has sharp fangs
- moves very quickly

Vervet monkey

- picks insects and dirt off each other
- eats fruits, plants, insects, and eggs

Warthog

- sleeps in holes lined with grass
- has bristles on its body

Oxpecker

- lays eggs in tree holes
- takes turns sitting on eggs

Yellow baboon

- eats grass, insects, and fish
- makes many sounds and even yawns

Zebra

- lives with a group called a herd
- has three species living in Africa

Africa

Atlantic Ocean

Indian Ocean

Words to Know

burrow (BUR-oh)—a hole or tunnel in the ground that is used by an animal; aardvarks live in burrows.

insect (IN-sekt)—a small animal with a hard outer shell, three body parts, six legs, and two antennas

pattern (PAT-urn)—a repeating set of colors, shapes, or figures

scale (SKALE)—one of the small pieces of hard skin that covers the body of a fish, snake, reptile, or other animal

Read More

Lee, Justin. *How to Draw African Animals.* A Kid's Guide to Drawing. New York: PowerKids Press, 2002.

Macken, JoAnn Early. *African Animals.* Animal Worlds. Milwaukee: Gareth Stevens, 2002.

Internet Sites

Track down many sites about African animals. Visit the FACT HOUND at *http://www.facthound.com*

IT IS EASY! IT IS FUN!

1) Go to *http://www.facthound.com*
2) Type in: 0736816798
3) Click on "FETCH IT" and FACT HOUND will find several links hand-picked by our editors.

Relax and let our pal FACT HOUND do the research for you!

Index

aardvark, 2

burrows, 2
bushbaby, 3

cheetah, 4
claws, 2, 7

dwarf mongoose, 5

elephant, 6, 25

fangs, 22
fish eagle, 7

giraffe, 8, 25

hippopotamus, 9
horns, 10, 12, 19

impala, 10

jackal, 11

kudu, 12

leaves, 8
lion, 13
lizards, 15

mountain gorilla, 14

necks, 8
Nile monitor, 15

ostrich, 16
oxpecker, 25

pangolin, 17
plants, 23

rhinoceros, 19

scales, 17
spotted hyena, 20
squacco heron, 18

termites, 2, 5
tongues, 2
tortoise, 21
trees, 3, 8, 12
tusks, 24

usambara tarantula, 22

vervet monkey, 23

warthog, 24
water, 7, 9, 15

yellow baboon, 26

zebra, 27

A+ Books are published by Capstone Press
P.O. Box 669, 151 Good Counsel Drive, Mankato, Minnesota 56002
http://www.capstone-press.com

1 2 3 4 5 6 08 07 06 05 04 03

Library of Congress Cataloging-in-Publication Data
Schuette, Sarah L., 1976–
    African animals ABC: an alphabet safari / by Sarah L. Schuette.
    p.cm.—(Alphabet Books)
    Includes bibliographical references and index.
    Summary: Introduces African animals through photographs and brief text that describe one animal for each letter of the alphabet.
    ISBN 0-7368-1679-8 (hardcover)
    1. Zoology—Africa—Juvenile literature. 2. English language—Alphabet—Juvenile literature.
[1. Zoology—Africa. 2. Animals. 3. Alphabet.] I. Title. 2. Series: Alphabet Books (Mankato, Minn.)
QL336 .S296 2003
591.96—dc21

2002015064

Credits
Heather Kindseth, designer; Juliette Peters, cover production; Deirdre Barton, photo researcher

Photo Credits
Corbis, cover, 7, 16, 25; Nigel J. Dennis, 2, 17; Lynda Richardson, 5; Theo Allofs, 10; Alissa Crandall, 11, 23, 24; Peter Johnson, 12, 18; Kevin Schafer, 14; David A. Northcott, 22
Digital Vision, 4, 13, 19, 21, 27
Image Ideas, Inc., 3, 8, 9, 15
J.C. Carton/Bruce Coleman Inc., 26
PhotoDisc, Inc., 6, 20

Note to Parents, Teachers, and Librarians

African Animals ABC uses color photographs and a nonfiction format to help children build mastery of the alphabet while learning about various animals that live in Africa. It is designed to be read aloud to a pre-reader or to be read independently by an early reader. The images help early readers and listeners understand the text and concepts discussed. The book encourages further learning by including the following sections: African Animal Facts, Words to Know, Read More, Internet Sites, and Index. Early readers may need assistance using these features.